Screen Kisses

Screen
Kisses

Quotes of Love,
Sex, and Romance
from the Movies

Compiled by
Ian Hardy and Gretchen Zufall

A Perigee Book

A Perigee Book
Published by The Berkley Publishing Group
200 Madison Avenue
New York, NY 10016

Copyright © 1997 by Hardy Justice and Gretchen Zufall
Book design by Maureen Troy
Cover design by James R. Harris
Cover photograph: *The Big Sleep*/Warner Bros. Pictures, Inc., 1946/The Kobal Collection

First edition: February 1997

Published simultaneously in Canada.

The Putnam Berkley World Wide Web site address is
http://www.berkley.com/berkley

Library of Congress Cataloging-in-Publication Data

Screen kisses : quotes of love, sex, and romance from the movies / compiled by Ian Hardy
    and Gretchen Zufall. —1st ed.
        p.   cm.
    ISBN 0-399-52270-0
    1. Motion pictures—Quotations, maxims, etc. 2. Love in motion pictures.
    3. Sex in motion pictures.   I. Hardy, Ian. II. Zufall, Gretchen.
    PN1994.9.S37   1997
    791.43'6538—dc20
                                                    96-19180
                                                    CIP

Printed in the United States of America

10 9 8 7 6 5 4 3 2 1

Screen Kisses

♥ ♥ ♥ ♥ ♥ ♥ Advice ♥ ♥ ♥ ♥ ♥ ♥

—Never take advice from someone of the opposite sex that doesn't know you intimately.

James Spader, SEX, LIES, AND VIDEOTAPE

—My mother told me to never enter any man's room in months ending in *r*.

Irene Dunne, LOVE AFFAIR

—If you're with a woman and she doesn't get it, she doesn't get what you're about, what's in your guts—move on.

John Spencer, FORGET PARIS

—Don't get mad. Get everything.

Ivana, THE FIRST WIVES CLUB

—Why don't you kiss her instead of talking her to death?

Irate neighbor to James Stewart, It's a WONDERFUL LIFE

♥ ♥ ♥ ♥ ♥ ♥ Age ♥ ♥ ♥ ♥ ♥ ♥

—My dear, when you're as old as I am, you take your men as you find them; that is, if you can find them.

Helen Broderick, TOP HAT

—When a girl's under twenty-one, she's protected by the law. When she's over sixty-five, she's protected by nature. Anywhere in between, she's fair game.

Cary Grant, OPERATION PETTICOAT

—What's fair about a man getting older and looking more distinguished and worldly and a woman getting older and looking old?

Dee Wallace, "10"

♥ ♥ ♥ ♥ ♥ ♥ Bad Boys ♥ ♥ ♥ ♥ ♥ ♥

—What I like about you is you're rock bottom. I wouldn't expect you to understand this, but it's a great comfort for a girl to know she could not possibly sink any lower.

Jane Greer to Robert Mitchum, THE BIG STEAL

—What is it about the wrong kind of man? In grade school it was guys with earrings. College: motorcycles, leather jackets. Now it's . . . black rubber.

Nicole Kidman to Val Kilmer, BATMAN FOREVER

—You're a real-life outlaw, aren't you?

—Well, I may be an outlaw, darling, but you're the one stealing my heart.

Geena Davis and Brad Pitt, THELMA & LOUISE

—Rick Von Sloneker is tall, rich, good-looking, stupid, dishonest, conceited, a bully, a liar, a drunk and a thief, an egomaniac, and probably psychotic . . . in short, completely attractive to women.

Christopher Eigeman, METROPOLITAN

—What do you know about scenery? Or beauty? Or any of the things that really make life worth living? You're just an animal—coarse, muscled, barbaric.

—You keep right on talking, honey. I like the way you run me down like that.

Barrie Chase and Robert Mitchum, CAPE FEAR

—Listen, if you don't want to lose that stardust look in your eyes, get going while the door's still open. You stick around here, you'll get grafters, shysters, two-bit thugs, and maybe worse—maybe me.

—I like those odds. I'm staying.

Mark Stevens and Lucille Ball, THE DARK CORNER

—What is there about a hoodlum that appeals to some women?

Cornel Wilde, THE BIG COMBO

—You know, you don't have to act with me, Steve. You don't have to say anything and you don't have to do anything. Not a thing. Oh, maybe just whistle. You know how to whistle, don't you, Steve? You just put your lips together and blow.

Lauren Bacall to Humphrey Bogart, TO HAVE AND HAVE NOT

—Well, I believe in the soul . . . The small of a woman's back. The hanging curve ball. High fiber. Good scotch. That the novels of Susan Sontag are self-indulgent, overrated crap. I believe that Lee Harvey Oswald acted alone. I believe there ought to be a constitutional amendment outlawing astroturf and the designated hitter. I believe in the sweet spot. Soft core pornography. Open your presents Christmas morning rather than Christmas Eve. And I believe in long, slow, deep, soft, wet kisses that last three days.

Kevin Costner to Susan Sarandon, BULL DURHAM

—Love don't make things nice. It ruins everything. It breaks your heart. It makes things a mess. We aren't here to make things perfect. The snowflakes are perfect. The stars are perfect. Not us. Not us. We are here to ruin ourselves and to break our hearts and love the wrong people and die. I mean the story books are bullshit. Now I want you to come upstairs with me and get in my bed!

Nicolas Cage to Cher, MOONSTRUCK

—I'd love to hold something the way you hold your guitar. That's the way I'd love to hold something, with such tender protection. I'd love to hold you that way—with that same tender protection. Because you hang the moon for me.

Joanne Woodward to Marlon Brando, THE FUGITIVE KIND

—You don't know what love means. To you, it's just another four-letter word.

Elizabeth Taylor to Paul Newman, CAT ON A HOT TIN ROOF

—I'm not livin' with you. We occupy the same cage, that's all.

Elizabeth Taylor to Paul Newman, CAT ON A HOT TIN ROOF

—Aren't you ever gonna stop deluding yourself? Behaving like some ludicrous little underage femme fatale. You're about as fatale as an after-dinner mint.

Michael York to Liza Minnelli, CABARET

—If you were my husband, I'd give you poison.
—If I were your husband, I'd take it.
   Margaret Hamilton and Billy Gilbert, PARADISE ALLEY

—You make me puke.
—That wasn't a very nice thing to say, Martha.
   Elizabeth Taylor and Richard Burton,
   WHO'S AFRAID OF VIRGINIA WOOLF?

—That's nice talk, Ben—keep drinking. Between the 101-proof breath and the occasional bits of drool, some interesting things come out.
   Elisabeth Shue to Nicolas Cage, LEAVING LAS VEGAS

♥ ♥ ♥ ♥ ♥ ♥ Body Parts ♥ ♥ ♥ ♥ ♥ ♥

—Sandy, your breasts feel weird.
—Oh, that's because they're real.

Steve Martin and Sarah Jessica Parker, L.A. STORY

—Are my breasts too small for you?
—Sometimes.

Bridget Fonda and Matt Dillon, SINGLES

—My problem is I'm both attracted and repelled by the male organ.

Diane Keaton, MANHATTAN

The Bonds of Matrimony

♥ ♥ ♥ ♥ ♥ ♥   ♥ ♥ ♥ ♥ ♥ ♥

—Marriage is punishment for shoplifting in some countries.

Mike Meyers, WAYNE'S WORLD

—Marriage for me is the death of hope.

Tony Roberts, A MIDSUMMER NIGHT'S SEX COMEDY

—I was always in the kitchen. I felt as though I'd been born in a kitchen and lived there all my life except for the few hours it took to get married.

Joan Crawford, MILDRED PIERCE

—A wedding is a funeral where you smell your own flowers.

—The bonds of matrimony can weigh heavily on one's soul.

♥ ♥ ♥ ♥ ♥ ♥ Boys' Night Out ♥ ♥ ♥ ♥ ♥ ♥

—Look, Charlie, we've got to get some girls. We've got to make a move. Even Gregory's at it now. We're falling behind. I don't think there's any advantage of putting it off any longer. Besides, it's making me depressed.

—When it came right down to it, I wasn't attracted to her.

—Should never stop you. Sometimes you got to say what the fuck. Make your move.

Tom Cruise and Richard Masur, RISKY BUSINESS

—You don't wanna get laid, man. It leads to kissing and pretty soon you gotta talk to 'em.

Sean Penn, COLORS

—They're all sisters. It's one big conspiracy. Trust me.

Michael Rapaport to Timothy Hutton, BEAUTIFUL GIRLS

—You know what your problem is: You're letting your head do too much of your thinking.

Jamie Foxx to Ben Chaplin, THE TRUTH ABOUT CATS & DOGS

♥ ♥ ♥ ♥ ♥ ♥ Breaking Up ♥ ♥ ♥ ♥ ♥ ♥

—Look, you've been submerged in another person's personality. Become a sub-person. And now you're free.

—Thanks a lot. Why didn't you tell me all of this before?

Patrick Malahide and Bill Paterson, COMFORT AND JOY

—There's something I want to tell you . . . I think I'm still in love with Yale.

—I'm stunned. I'm in a state of, uh . . . somebody should throw a blanket over me.

Diane Keaton and Woody Allen, ANNIE HALL

♥ ♥ ♥ ♥ ♥ ♥ Broken Hearts ♥ ♥ ♥ ♥ ♥ ♥

—Who was the girl, Steve?

—What girl?

—The one who left you with such a high opinion of women. She must have been quite a gal.

Lauren Bacall and Humphrey Bogart, TO HAVE AND HAVE NOT

—I worshiped her.

—That's not the nicest thing you can do to somebody, is it? I hope you don't worship me.

—No, you're my friend.

Bill Paterson and Patrick Malahide, COMFORT AND JOY

—You musn't give your heart to wild things. The more you do, the stronger they get. Until they're strong enough to run into the woods or fly into a tree and then a higher tree and then to the sky.

Audrey Hepburn, BREAKFAST AT TIFFANY'S

—How many days did we have? Mostly I remember the last one, the wild finish. A guy standing on the station platform in the rain with a comical look on his face because his insides have been kicked out.

Humphrey Bogart to Ingrid Bergman, CASABLANCA

—It took more than one man to change my name to "Shanghai Lily."

Marlene Dietrich, SHANGHAI EXPRESS

—Maybe I'll live so long that I'll forget her. Maybe I'll die trying.

Orson Welles, THE LADY FROM SHANGHAI

—Of all the gin joints, in all the towns, in all the world, she walks into mine.

Humphrey Bogart, CASABLANCA

—The sun's gone down and the moon has turned black, for I loved him and he didn't love back.

Jennifer Jason Leigh, MRS. PARKER AND THE VICIOUS CIRCLE

♥ ♥ ♥ ♥ ♥ ♥ The Chase ♥ ♥ ♥ ♥ ♥ ♥

—Why do you suppose we only feel compelled to chase the ones who run away?

John Malkovich, DANGEROUS LIAISONS

—Why do men chase women?
—Nerves?
—I think it's because they fear death.

Olympia Dukakis and John Mahoney, MOONSTRUCK

—My plumber tells me that the pursuit of women is flight from women.

—What does that mean?

—How the hell do I know? Am I a plumber?

Walter Matthau and Carol Burnett, PETE 'N' TILLIE

♥ ♥ ♥ ♥ ♥ ♥ Chastity ♥ ♥ ♥ ♥ ♥ ♥

—There are worse things than chastity.

—Yes . . . lunacy and death.

Deborah Kerr and Richard Burton, THE NIGHT OF THE IGUANA

—She's gonna spend the rest of her life saying, "I'm not that kind of girl." I'm only afraid that someday before she can finish saying it, she will be.

Audrey Meadows, THAT TOUCH OF MINK

—We're fighting for this woman's honor, which is more than she ever did.

Groucho Marx, DUCK SOUP

—Mother, this is why I've had to spend half my life traveling around the world after you. To keep men like this away from you.

—Well, after this, let me run my own interference. Seems like the blockers are having all the fun.

Grace Kelly and Jessie Royce Ladis, TO CATCH A THIEF

♥ ♥ ♥ ♥ ♥ ♥ Cold Feet ♥ ♥ ♥ ♥ ♥ ♥

—I keep thinking I'm going to be missing out on things, you know?

—Yeah, well, that's what marriage is all about.

Steve Guttenberg and Mickey Rourke, DINER

—When men get around me, they get allergic to wedding rings.

Eve Arden, MILDRED PIERCE

—I'm just trying to understand why you don't want to marry someone you love.

—Because it doesn't work. Marriage doesn't work. You know, what works is divorce.

—Divorce is only a temporary solution.

Maureen Stapleton and Meryl Streep, HEARTBURN

♥ ♥ ♥ ♥ ♥ ♥ Come-Ons ♥ ♥ ♥ ♥ ♥ ♥

—Life is very long and full of salesmanship, Miss Clara. You might buy something yet.

Paul Newman to Joanne Woodward, THE LONG HOT SUMMER

—I seem to remember you from one of my dreams.
One of the better ones.
Dick Powell to Anne Shirley, FAREWELL, MY LOVELY

—I've a head for business and a bod for sin.
Melanie Griffith to Harrison Ford, WORKING GIRL

—Shall I take you somewhere else?
—You're going to find it very easy to take me anywhere.
Robert Mitchum and Jane Greer, OUT OF THE PAST

—That's a honey of an anklet you're wearing, Mrs.
Dietrichson.
Fred MacMurray to Barbara Stanwyck, DOUBLE INDEMNITY

♥ ♥ ♥ ♥ ♥ ♥ Commitment ♥ ♥ ♥ ♥ ♥ ♥

—I have never had sex with someone that I loved before.

Ethan Hawke, REALITY BITES

—If I say that I do have difficulty with duality, you're going to think I'm a Norman Bates/Ted Bundy type and, well, you might not let me kiss you.

—It's the so-called normal guys that always let you down. Sickos never scare me. At least they're committed.

Michael Keaton and Michelle Pfeiffer, BATMAN RETURNS

—Why is it when a relationship doesn't work, we say it's because he can't commit? Don't I bear some of the blame here?

Mira Sorvino to girlfriends, BEAUTIFUL GIRLS

♥ ♥ ♥ ♥ ♥ ♥ Dating ♥ ♥ ♥ ♥ ♥ ♥

—Things are a little different now. First, you have to be friends. You have to like each other. Then, you neck. This could go on for years. Then you have tests, and then you get to do it with a condom. The good news is you split the check.

Rob Reiner to Tom Hanks, SLEEPLESS IN SEATTLE

—What are you doing Saturday night?
—Committing suicide.
—What are you doing Friday night?

Woody Allen and Diana Davila, PLAY IT AGAIN, SAM

—We spend hours making ourselves look completely different, and then we go into some dark place where we really can't see each other anyway, and then we drink so we don't know if the other person is really interesting or just seems interesting 'cause they're pretending to be interested in the person that we're pretending to be.

—Uh, right. So I guess there's no getting around it. We're gonna have to lie to each other.

Teri Polo and Ethan Hawke, MYSTERY DATE

♥ ♥ ♥ ♥ ♥ ♥ Declarations of ♥ ♥ ♥ ♥ ♥ ♥ Love

—I feel really goofy saying this, after only knowing you one night and me being a call girl and all, but I think `I love you.

Patricia Arquette to Christian Slater, TRUE ROMANCE

—Until I met you, I had only ever experienced desire, love never.

John Malkovich to Michelle Pfeiffer, DANGEROUS LIAISONS

—I'm in love with you.
—Snap out of it!

Nicolas Cage and Cher, MOONSTRUCK

—I love you. You belong to me.
—No, people don't belong to people.
—Of course they do.

George Peppard and Audrey Hepburn,
BREAKFAST AT TIFFANY'S

—In the words of David Cassidy, in fact, while he was still with the Partridge Family, I think I love you.

Hugh Grant to Andie MacDowell,
FOUR WEDDINGS AND A FUNERAL

♥ ♥ ♥ ♥ ♥ ♥ Desperation ♥ ♥ ♥ ♥ ♥ ♥

—Wouldn't this be a great world if insecurity and desperation made us more attractive?
Albert Brooks, BROADCAST NEWS

—Desperation . . . it's the world's worst cologne.
Sheila Kelley, SINGLES

♥ ♥ ♥ ♥ ♥ ♥ Differences Between Sexes ♥ ♥ ♥ ♥ ♥ ♥

—Men marry because they are tired, women marry because they are curious, and both are disappointed.
George Sanders, THE PICTURE OF DORIAN GRAY

—Women need a reason to have sex; men just need a place.

Billy Crystal, CITY SLICKERS

—Men learn to love what they're attracted to, whereas women become more and more attracted to the person they love.

James Spader, SEX, LIES, AND VIDEOTAPE

—Men enjoy the happiness they feel. We can only enjoy the happiness we give. They're not capable of devoting themselves exclusively to one person, so to hope to be made happy by love is a certain cause of grief.

Mildred Natwick, DANGEROUS LIAISONS

♥ ♥ ♥ ♥ ♥ ♥ Dirty Old Men ♥ ♥ ♥ ♥ ♥ ♥

—Once a month, I try to make pretty young girls nervous, just to keep my ego from going out.
> Charles Boyer to Jane Fonda, BAREFOOT IN THE PARK

—She's twenty-five years old. Her skin is like a ribbon of candy. Breasts like sponge cake. Her calves are like calzone—highly edible . . . she's crazy about sex. This is somebody getting me over the rough spots.
> Jeff Goldblum to Hugh Grant, NINE MONTHS

♥ ♥ ♥ ♥ ♥ ♥ Divorce ♥ ♥ ♥ ♥ ♥ ♥

—Why did you keep his name?
—It's the only thing he was giving away.
> George Segal and Glenda Jackson, A TOUCH OF CLASS

—I was married to him for eight months; I gave him the best years of my life.
Divorcée, THE BIG BROADCAST OF 1938

—Look at the facts.
—I know, I know. Fifty percent of all marriages end in divorce.
—Not to mention the ones that end in gunplay.
Gil Bellows and Sarah Jessica Parker, MIAMI RHAPSODY

♥ ♥ ♥ ♥ ♥ Dogs ♥ ♥ ♥ ♥ ♥ ♥

—I think all men are dogs. All men start barking sooner or later.
Octavia Saint Laurent, PARIS IS BURNING

—Oh, men. I never yet met one of them who didn't have the instincts of a heel.

Eve Arden, MILDRED PIERCE

—I'd say she's doing a woman's hardest job: juggling wolves.

Grace Kelly watching party girl in building next door, REAR WINDOW

—I married a liar. Why? Because I married a man.

Bonnie Hunt, ONLY YOU

—I never trust men that are too charming—that's why I married you.

June Haver to William Lundigan, LOVE NEST

—I don't know why Dione is going out with a high school boy. They're like dogs. You have to clean them and feed them and they're just like these nervous creatures that jump and slobber over you.

Alicia Silverstone, CLUELESS

♥ ♥ ♥ ♥ ♥ ♥ The Doldrums ♥ ♥ ♥ ♥ ♥ ♥

—Marriage is when a woman asks a man to remove his pajamas because she wants to send them to the laundry.

Albert Finney, TWO FOR THE ROAD

—It's hard to believe that you haven't had sex in two hundred years.

—Two hundred and four if you count my marriage.

Diane Keaton and Woody Allen, SLEEPER

—Are you sexually active?
—I'd say I'm experiencing a dry spell.
—So, you're married?

Lisa Banes and Sarah Jessica Parker, MIAMI RHAPSODY

—At the rate we're having sex we may as well be married already.

Geena Davis, EARTH GIRLS ARE EASY

—I can hardly wait until we're married.
—Why?
—Because then I'll never have to have sex with you again.

Meg Tilly and Eric Stoltz, SLEEP WITH ME

♥ ♥ ♥ ♥ ♥ ♥ Drunk with Love ♥ ♥ ♥ ♥ ♥ ♥

— Two [drinks], I'm anybody's.
— Three, and I'm everybody's.
— Four, and I'm nobody's.
  John Polson, Russell Crowe, and Jack Thompson,
  THE SUM OF US

— I am a drunk, and you're a hooker. I am a person who is totally at ease with this.
  Nicolas Cage to Elisabeth Shue, LEAVING LAS VEGAS

♥ ♥ ♥ ♥ ♥ ♥ Dry Spells ♥ ♥ ♥ ♥ ♥ ♥

— The last time I was inside a woman was when I visited the Statue of Liberty.
  Woody Allen, CRIMES AND MISDEMEANORS

—I truly believe that if we can get two women on the Supreme Court, we can get at least one on you.

Janeane Garofalo to Steve Zahn, REALITY BITES

♥ ♥ ♥ ♥ ♥ ♥ End of the Affair ♥ ♥ ♥ ♥ ♥ ♥

—Why is it that we don't always recognize the moment that love begins? We always know when it ends.

Steve Martin, L.A. STORY

—You know what's weird. You never know the last time you sleep with somebody that it's the last time. You're thinking, oh, we've got problems, we've got work to do, you know, but you never think . . . And then you break up and a month later you look back and you go, oh, that was it. That Tuesday or Friday or whatever, and you wish you paid attention because it was the last time.

Mary-Louise Parker, BOYS ON THE SIDE

♥ ♥ ♥ ♥ ♥ ♥ Excuses ♥ ♥ ♥ ♥ ♥ ♥

—I never touched her. I mean, I touched her. She touched me, but that was all. Nothing happened.

Wallace Shawn,
SCENES FROM THE CLASS STRUGGLE IN BEVERLY HILLS

—You know, the first man that can think up a good explanation how he can be in love with his wife and another woman is going to win that prize they're always giving out in Sweden.

Mary Cecil, THE WOMEN

♥♥♥♥♥♥ Expressions of ♥♥♥♥♥♥
Lust

—She was giving me the kind of look I could feel in my hip pocket.

Dick Powell, FAREWELL, MY LOVELY

—I got to meet that girl. She is death.

Mickey Rourke, DINER

—That bass player's a babe. She makes me feel kind of funny—like when we used to climb the rope in gym class.

Dana Carvey, WAYNE'S WORLD

—Schwing.
 Mike Meyers and Dana Carvey, WAYNE'S WORLD

♥ ♥ ♥ ♥ ♥ ♥   Fate   ♥ ♥ ♥ ♥ ♥ ♥

—Maybe it's just the timing, but I feel like I would go anywhere with you. We mustn't hurry into things . . . No, can't hurry things any more than we can stop them.
 Greta Scacchi to Tim Robbins, THE PLAYER

—Why didn't we do this before?
—Because it was always going to be this hard to stop.
 Michelle Pfeiffer and Robert Redford,
 UP CLOSE AND PERSONAL

—Dad, I was talking to Jessica about reincarnation. She says you knew Annie in another life.

—Who's Annie?

—The one who wrote us. But Jessica says you and Annie never got together in that life. So your hearts are like puzzles with missing pieces—and when you get together, the puzzle's complete. The reason I know this and you don't is because I'm younger and pure. So I'm more in touch with cosmic forces.

Eight-year-old Ross Malinger and Tom Hanks,
SLEEPLESS IN SEATTLE

—Destiny is something we've invented because we can't stand the fact that everything that happens is accidental.

Meg Ryan, SLEEPLESS IN SEATTLE

—I know what you're thinking. We made the connection. And when you make the connection, it, like chemistry, takes care of itself. I mean, it makes its own decisions, you know. So you just got to sit back and enjoy it, because you know when it's real and this is real. And we just don't have to discuss it.

—Janet, you're spazzing off on me.

Bridget Fonda and Matt Dillon, SINGLES

♥ ♥ ♥ ♥ ♥ ♥ Femme Fatales ♥ ♥ ♥ ♥ ♥ ♥

—I don't do murder.
—You would if you loved me.

Peter Berg and Linda Fiorentino, THE LAST SEDUCTION

—She liked me. I could feel that. The way you feel when the cards are falling right for you, with a nice little pile of blue and yellow chips in the middle of the table. Only what I didn't know then was that I wasn't playing her. She was playing me, with a deck of marked cards, and the stakes weren't any blue and yellow chips. They were dynamite.

Fred MacMurray, DOUBLE INDEMNITY

—You're not too bright. I like that in a man.
Kathleen Turner to William Hurt, BODY HEAT

—I never saw her in the daytime. We seemed to live by night. What was left of the day went away like a pack of cigarettes you smoked.
Robert Mitchum, OUT OF THE PAST

—Honey, if I couldn't get a man to leave her, I wouldn't kill him. I'd kill myself.

Sharon Stone to Kathy Bates, DIABOLIQUE

♥ ♥ ♥ ♥ ♥ ♥ Fickle Hearts ♥ ♥ ♥ ♥ ♥ ♥

—A few minutes ago, I liked Hugo better; now I like you better. It's funny how men change.

Shirley Temple to Cary Grant,
THE BACHELOR AND THE BOBBY-SOXER

—Only last night you were ready to give up everything for me.

—Well, that was last night, you know. People say things they don't mean sometimes at night. Life is something besides kisses and promises and the moonlight. Even you should know that.

Robert Taylor and Greta Garbo, CAMILLE

—This is a very strange love affair.
—Why?
—Maybe the fact that you don't love me.
  Ingrid Bergman and Cary Grant, NOTORIOUS

♥ ♥ ♥ ♥ ♥ ♥ First Dates ♥ ♥ ♥ ♥ ♥ ♥

—Ordinarily I don't like to be around interesting people because it means I have to be interesting, too.
—Are you saying I'm interesting?
—All I'm saying is that when I'm around you I find myself showing off, which is the idiot's version of being interesting.
  Steve Martin and Victoria Tennant, L.A. STORY

—Don't you hate that?

—What?

—Uncomfortable silences. Why do we feel it's necessary to yak about bullshit in order to be comfortable?

—I don't know.

—That's when you know you've found somebody special. When you can just shut the fuck up for a minute, and comfortably share silence.

—I don't think we're there yet. But don't feel bad, we just met each other.

Uma Thurman and John Travolta, PULP FICTION

—Do you want to come in?

—More than I want the ascot to come back in style, but not tonight.

Gabrielle Anwar and Andy Garcia,
THINGS TO DO IN DENVER WHEN YOU'RE DEAD

—Tonight has been so perfect. Let's wait for another night to screw it up.

Janeane Garofalo to Ben Chaplin,
THE TRUTH ABOUT CATS & DOGS

♥ ♥ ♥ ♥ ♥ ♥ First Times ♥ ♥ ♥ ♥ ♥ ♥

—You'll find the shame is like the pain. You only feel it once.

Glenn Close to Uma Thurman, DANGEROUS LIAISONS

—I was eighteen: Jeff the jock, my basement, Valentine's Day, *Jeopardy* in the background. Jeff said it would last longer with the show on to distract him. He got all the answers wrong except sports. By Double Jeopardy, he was done. By Final Jeopardy, he was on his way home.

Meg Ryan, FRENCH KISS

—Did we, uhm?

—Yeah, I'm pretty sure.

—Excuse me, do you know if I enjoyed it? What am I—nuts? Of course I enjoyed it. What I meant was, did you?

—You know, I have this weird feeling I did.

Anthony Michael Hall and Haviland Morris, SIXTEEN CANDLES

❤ ❤ ❤ ❤ ❤ ❤ Flirting ❤ ❤ ❤ ❤ ❤ ❤

—I don't bite, you know—unless it's called for.

Audrey Hepburn, CHARADE

—You're not that great looking.

—I know, but can I help it if you think so?

Ryan O'Neal and Ali MacGraw, LOVE STORY

—Go home with me.

—No.

—Well, to be perfectly honest with you, I don't find you the least bit attractive . . . Now you want to go home with me?

Timothy Hutton and Uma Thurman, BEAUTIFUL GIRLS

—All night long I've had the most terrible impulse to do something.

—Never resist an impulse . . . Especially if it's terrible.

Audrey Hepburn and Humphrey Bogart, SABRINA

—Do you know what's wrong with you?

—No, what?

—Nothing.

Audrey Hepburn and Cary Grant, CHARADE

♥ ♥ ♥ ♥ ♥ ♥ Flying Solo ♥ ♥ ♥ ♥ ♥ ♥

— Don't knock masturbation. It's sex with someone I love.

Woody Allen, ANNIE HALL

— Have a wank, have a wank? I just can't have a wank. I need three days' notice to have a wank. You can just stand there and do it. Me, it's like organizing D-day. Forces have to be assembled. Magazines bought. The past dredged for some suitably unsavory episode, the dogged thought of which can still produce a faint flicker of desire. Have a wank? Be easier to raise the *Titanic*.

Alfred Molina, PRICK UP YOUR EARS

—I was naughty all day yesterday.
—Not with me, you weren't.
—You'll just have to learn to show up on time.
Michael Caine and Maggie Smith, CALIFORNIA SUITE

—Time sure flies when you're young and jerking off.
Leonardo Di Caprio, THE BASKETBALL DIARIES

♥ ♥ ♥ ♥ ♥ ♥ Fooling Around ♥ ♥ ♥ ♥ ♥ ♥

—I'm a married woman.
—Meaning what?
—Meaning I'm not looking for company.
—Then you should have said happily married.
Kathleen Turner and William Hurt, BODY HEAT

—Aren't you forgetting that you're married?
—I'm doing my best.
Dick Foran and Mae West, MY LITTLE CHICKADEE

—Pardon me, but your husband is showing.
Glenn Ford, GILDA

—Last time I looked, you had a wife.
—Maybe next time you look, I won't.
—That's what they all say.
Barbara Stanwyck and Robert Ryan, CLASH BY NIGHT

—I've respected your husband for many years, and what's good enough for him is good enough for me.
Groucho Marx, MONKEY BUSINESS

—Are you married, George?
—Not usually.
Ann Wedgeworth and Gerard Depardieu, GREEN CARD

♥ ♥ ♥ ♥ ♥ ♥ Foreplay ♥ ♥ ♥ ♥ ♥ ♥

—A guy'll listen to anything if he thinks it's foreplay.
Susan Sarandon, BULL DURHAM

♥ ♥ ♥ ♥ ♥ ♥ Frequency ♥ ♥ ♥ ♥ ♥ ♥

Psychiatrist: How often do you sleep together?
— Hardly ever, maybe three times a week.
— Constantly, I'd say three times a week.
  Woody Allen and Diane Keaton, ANNIE HALL

— We barely have sex once a week.
— So . . . If we were married that would put us like in
the ninety-eighth percentile.
  Gil Bellows and Sarah Jessica Parker, MIAMI RHAPSODY

♥ ♥ ♥ ♥ ♥ ♥ Fresh Talk ♥ ♥ ♥ ♥ ♥ ♥

—This may come as a shock to you, but there are some men who don't end every sentence with a proposition.

Doris Day to Rock Hudson, PILLOW TALK

♥ ♥ ♥ ♥ ♥ ♥ Friendship ♥ ♥ ♥ ♥ ♥ ♥

—I wonder if we were really friends with them at all . . . or whether we were just weigh stations between dates, you know. For them, men are either dates, potential dates, or date substitutes. I find that dehumanizing.

Bryan Leder, METROPOLITAN

—Friendship's a lot more lasting than love.

—Yeah, but not as entertaining.

Joan Crawford and Jack Carson, MILDRED PIERCE

—No man can be friends with a woman he finds attractive. He always wants to have sex with her.

—So you are saying that a man can be friends with a woman he finds unattractive?

—No, you pretty much want to nail them, too.

Billy Crystal and Meg Ryan, WHEN HARRY MET SALLY . . .

♥ ♥ ♥ ♥ ♥ ♥ Gigolos ♥ ♥ ♥ ♥ ♥ ♥

—Boys like you don't work.

—What do you mean, boys like me?

—Ones that play the guitar and go around talking about how warm they are.

—That happens to be the truth. My temperature's always a couple of degrees above normal, the same as a dog's.

Anna Magnani and Marlon Brando, THE FUGITIVE KIND

—People who are very beautiful make their own laws.

Vivien Leigh, THE ROMAN SPRING OF MRS. STONE

—Well, I'll tell you the truth now. I ain't a real cowboy, but I am one hell of a stud.

Jon Voight, MIDNIGHT COWBOY

♥ ♥ ♥ ♥ ♥ ♥ Girl Talk ♥ ♥ ♥ ♥ ♥ ♥

—I refuse to go out with a man whose ass is smaller than mine.

> Elizabeth Perkins to Demi Moore, "ABOUT LAST NIGHT . . ."

—You could park a car in the shadow of his ass.

> Geena Davis, THELMA & LOUISE

—I wonder what kind of a build he's got on him.

—Did you ever see his feet? I heard one time that that's supposed to be an indication.

> Lelia Goldoni and Ellen Burstyn,
> ALICE DOESN'T LIVE HERE ANYMORE

—Look at his basket. Hard as a steel baguette.

> Mary Woronov,
> SCENES FROM THE CLASS STRUGGLE IN BEVERLY HILLS

♥ ♥ ♥ ♥ ♥ ♥ Gold-Digging ♥ ♥ ♥ ♥ ♥ ♥

—I wasn't always rich. There was a time when I didn't know where my next husband was coming from.
Mae West, SHE DONE HIM WRONG

—You're the only girl in the world that can stand on a stage with a spotlight in her eye and still see a diamond inside a man's pocket.
Jane Russell to Marilyn Monroe, GENTLEMEN PREFER BLONDES

—If we can't empty his pockets between us, we're not worthy of the name "woman."
Jane Russell to Marilyn Monroe, GENTLEMEN PREFER BLONDES

—I mean, any gentleman with the slightest chic will give a girl a fifty-dollar bill for the powder room.
Audrey Hepburn, BREAKFAST AT TIFFANY'S

—I really do love Gus. There's not another millionaire in the world with such a gentle disposition.

Marilyn Monroe to Jane Russell, Gentlemen Prefer Blondes

—You're here in Europe to buy a husband.
—The man I want doesn't have a price.
—Well, that eliminates me.

Cary Grant and Grace Kelly, To Catch a Thief

—You must all be so rich.
—Well, we aren't exactly poor.
—Julia, you should have told me, you really should.
—Would it have made any difference?
—Certainly, I would have asked you to marry me in two days instead of ten.

Cary Grant and Doris Nolan, Holiday

—Nobody poor was ever called democratic for marrying somebody rich.

Walter Hampden, SABRINA

♥♥♥♥♥♥ Happily Ever After ♥♥♥♥♥♥

—Let's be sensible. We're happy now; if we get married we'll ruin everything. The minute you get married you start to drive each other crazy.

—That will never happen with us.

—Why not?

—Because you already drive me crazy.

Meryl Streep and Jack Nicholson, HEARTBURN

—I never felt that true love should stand in the way of a good time.

Anne Bancroft, TO BE OR NOT TO BE

—What you probably feel is the melancholy of happiness. That mood that comes over all of us when we realize that even love can't remain a flood tide forever.

Lionel Barrymore to Greta Garbo, CAMILLE

—I'm afraid after we've been married awhile a beautiful young girl will come along and you'll forget all about me.

—Don't be silly, I'll write you once a week.

Margaret Dumont and Groucho Marx, THE BIG STORE

The Honeymoon's Over

♥ ♥ ♥ ♥ ♥ ♥   ♥ ♥ ♥ ♥ ♥ ♥

—When you want to make out, who do you make out to: Sinatra or Mathis?

—I'm married. We don't make out.

Paul Reiser and Daniel Stern, DINER

—Marriage can't work when one person is happy and the other person is miserable. Marriage is both people being equally miserable.

Joe Mantegna, FORGET PARIS

—The honeymoon is over. It's time to get married.

Carol Burnett to Walter Matthau, PETE 'N' TILLY

Hopeless
Romantics

♥ ♥ ♥ ♥ ♥ ♥   ♥ ♥ ♥ ♥ ♥ ♥

—You're still the chauffeur's daughter, and you're still reaching for the moon.

—No, father, the moon is reaching for me.

Walter Hampden and Audrey Hepburn, SABRINA

—You're worse than a hopeless romantic. You're a hopeful one.

Jane Fonda to Alan Alda, CALIFORNIA SUITE

—Why can't anything be perfect?

Greta Garbo to Laura Hope Crews, CAMILLE

—A kiss may not be the truth, but it is what we wish
were true.
Steve Martin, L.A. STORY

♥ ♥ ♥ ♥ ♥ ♥ Impossible ♥ ♥ ♥ ♥ ♥ ♥
Situations

—You're an alien and I'm from the Valley.
Geena Davis to extraterrestrial Jeff Goldblum,
EARTH GIRLS ARE EASY

—All my life I've been waiting for someone, and when
I find her, she's a fish.
Tom Hanks on finding out Daryl Hannah is a mermaid, SPLASH

—It never pays to get mixed up with human beings.
Jack Lemmon on witch Kim Novak falling in love with human
James Stewart, BELL, BOOK AND CANDLE

♥ ♥ ♥ ♥ ♥ ♥ Infatuation ♥ ♥ ♥ ♥ ♥ ♥

—It was like electricity.

—I know, that wonderful AC/DC feeling, but that's not love.

—Oh, it's close enough.
Jayne Mansfield and Joan Blondell,
WILL SUCCESS SPOIL ROCK HUNTER?

—I met this woman, this apparition, this goddess.

—Goddess?

—It's French for goddess. And so is she, Kate. She's French. I've never felt this way before. I could do anything. I could rule the world. Climb the highest mountain. I could walk into the men's room and pee with some big guy waiting in line behind me.

Timothy Hutton and Meg Ryan, FRENCH KISS

—She's a fox.

—She's a babe.

—She's a robo-babe.

—If she were a president, she'd be Babraham Lincoln.

Mike Meyers and Dana Carvey, WAYNE'S WORLD

♥ ♥ ♥ ♥ ♥ ♥ Infidelity ♥ ♥ ♥ ♥ ♥ ♥

—Your idea of fidelity is not having more than one man in the bed at the same time.
Dirk Bogarde to Julie Christie, DARLING

—The only question I've ever asked any woman is what time is your husband coming home.
Paul Newman, HUD

—I'm so disappointed in you. It's so damned unoriginal. Everyone cheats with their secretary; I expected more from my husband.
Maureen Stapleton, PLAZA SUITE

—We've been married for eleven years and not once have I been unfaithful to her in the same city.

George Segal, A TOUCH OF CLASS

—What are we going to do?

—You're taken care of, you're having an affair. I'm the one who needs an activity.

Walter Matthau and Maureen Stapleton, PLAZA SUITE

—Why is it, the only time a wife knows how you feel is when you feel it for another woman?

Unidentified, HOW TO SAVE A MARRIAGE (AND RUIN YOUR LIFE)

—What most wives fail to realize is that their husbands' philandering has nothing whatever to do with them.

John Halliday, THE PHILADELPHIA STORY

—Don't be so naive. Your father has been unfaithful plenty of times.

—You couldn't get back at him the old-fashioned way? You know, you just go crazy with his credit card or something?

Mia Farrow and Sarah Jessica Parker, discussing
Farrow's affair, MIAMI RHAPSODY

♥ ♥ ♥ ♥ ♥ ♥ Inhibitions ♥ ♥ ♥ ♥ ♥ ♥

—Oh, inhibitions are always nice because they're so nice to overcome.

Jane Fonda, KLUTE

—You have no cards. Why did you call?

—I felt like it.

—Playing strip poker with an exhibitionist somehow takes the challenge away.

Christopher Eigeman and Isabel Gillies, METROPOLITAN

♥ ♥ ♥ ♥ ♥ ♥ In the Heat of the Moment ♥ ♥ ♥ ♥ ♥ ♥

—But you were sexy, you know. You were all soaking wet from the rain, and I had a mad impulse to throw you down on the lunar surface and commit interstellar perversion with you.

Woody Allen, MANHATTAN

—So, let's do it.

—With all the lights on?

—Yeah, right here on the oriental. With all the lights on.

Anjelica Huston and Jack Nicholson, PRIZZI'S HONOR

—I don't make too much noise.

—No, no, I love all that screaming. It makes me feel like Michael Bolton.

Carla Gugino and Bo Eason, MIAMI RHAPSODY

♥ ♥ ♥ ♥ ♥ ♥ Jaded ♥ ♥ ♥ ♥ ♥ ♥

—Love is an intoxication.

—And marriage is the hangover.

Bit player and Bert Wheeler, CRACKED NUTS

—True love is like the Loch Ness monster—everyone has heard of it, but no one's ever seen it.

Meshach Taylor, MANNEQUIN TWO: ON THE MOVE

—I think I'm in love with you, too, Charlie.

—Not in love. In love is temporary, then you move on to the next in love. Everybody's always falling in and out of love. I know this. I read about it in the magazines. When you're just in love, it's just a hormonal secretion which changes the sense of smell so as to affect somebody in a certain way. That's what in love is. Who needs it?

Jack Nicholson and Kathleen Turner, PRIZZI'S HONOR

—I shall love Armand always. And I believe he shall love me always, too.

—Hasn't your own experience taught you the human heart can't be trusted?

Greta Garbo and Lionel Barrymore, CAMILLE

♥ ♥ ♥ ♥ ♥ ♥ Jail Bait ♥ ♥ ♥ ♥ ♥ ♥

—Have you ever noticed, the older you get, the younger your girlfriends get? Soon, you'll be dating sperm.

Billy Crystal, CITY SLICKERS

—Eighteen. Is there any word in the English language as sexy as that?

Robin Williams, THE WORLD ACCORDING TO GARP

—I'm forty-two and she's seventeen. I'm dating a girl wherein I can beat up her father. It's the first time that phenomenon ever occurred in my life.

Woody Allen, MANHATTAN

♥ ♥ ♥ ♥ ♥ ♥ Jealousy ♥ ♥ ♥ ♥ ♥ ♥

—How did he know you were here?
—Well you do, don't you? In that state, you know everything.
Vanessa Redgrave and Gary Oldman, PRICK UP YOUR EARS

—I don't believe in jealousy. It's dumb. One thing though: touch his dick and he's dead.
Kevin Kline, A FISH CALLED WANDA

♥ ♥ ♥ ♥ ♥ ♥ Kinky Sex ♥ ♥ ♥ ♥ ♥ ♥

—I like to watch.
Peter Sellers, BEING THERE

—I'd like to try it in your house sometime. The idea of doing it in my sister's bed gives me a perverse thrill.

Laura San Giacomo, SEX, LIES, AND VIDEOTAPE

—I used to make obscene phone calls to her collect— and she used to accept the charges.

Woody Allen, TAKE THE MONEY AND RUN

—I looked for you in my closet tonight.

Isabella Rossellini, BLUE VELVET

—We were only hurting each other.
—I thought that's the way you wanted it.

Valeria Golino and Cary Elwes, HOT SHOTS!

♥ ♥ ♥ ♥ ♥ ♥ Kissing ♥ ♥ ♥ ♥ ♥ ♥

—Yes, I will say you do things with dispatch. No wasted preliminaries. Not only did I enjoy that kiss last night, I was awed by the efficiency of it.

—Well, I'm a great believer in getting down to essentials.

Cary Grant and Grace Kelly, TO CATCH A THIEF

—It's even better when you help.

Lauren Bacall to Humphrey Bogart, TO HAVE AND HAVE NOT

—My plan was to kiss her with every lip on my face.

Steve Martin, DEAD MEN DON'T WEAR PLAID

—I like that—except for the beard. Why don't you shave and we'll try it again.

Lauren Bacall to Humphrey Bogart, TO HAVE AND HAVE NOT

—I don't know how to kiss, or I would kiss you. Where do the noses go?

Ingrid Bergman to Gary Cooper, FOR WHOM THE BELL TOLLS

♥ ♥ ♥ ♥ ♥ ♥ Kiss Me Deadly ♥ ♥ ♥ ♥ ♥ ♥

—Kiss me, Mike. I want you to kiss me. Kiss me. The liar's kiss that says I love you and means something else.

Gaby Rodgers to Ralph Meeker, KISS ME DEADLY

—When we get home, Frank, then there'll be kisses, kisses with life and not death.

Lana Turner to John Garfield,
THE POSTMAN ALWAYS RINGS TWICE

—You should be kissed, and often, and by someone
who knows how.
Clark Gable to Vivien Leigh, GONE WITH THE WIND

♥ ♥ ♥ ♥ ♥ ♥   Liars   ♥ ♥ ♥ ♥ ♥ ♥

—The next time you have the need to say "I love you"
to someone, say it to yourself—and see if you believe it.
Harvey Fierstein, TORCH SONG TRILOGY

—I never said I love you. I don't care about I love you.
I read the *Second Sex*. I read *The Cinderella Complex*. I'm
responsible for my own orgasm. I don't care. I just don't
want to be lied to.
Teri Garr, TOOTSIE

♥ ♥ ♥ ♥ ♥ ♥ Lines ♥ ♥ ♥ ♥ ♥ ♥

—I'd know you anytime, anyplace, anywhere.
Cary Grant to Rosalind Russell, HIS GIRL FRIDAY

—Flattery will get you anywhere.
Jane Russell, GENTLEMEN PREFER BLONDES

—Is that a gun in your pocket or are you just pleased
to see me?
Mae West, SHE DONE HIM WRONG

—I never liked a man I didn't meet.
Jennifer Jason Leigh, MRS. PARKER AND THE VICIOUS CIRCLE

—It's the car, right? Chicks love the car.
Val Kilmer to Nicole Kidman, BATMAN FOREVER

♥ ♥ ♥ ♥ ♥ ♥ Logistics ♥ ♥ ♥ ♥ ♥ ♥

—You can't make love on wet sand . . . it just gets into everything.
Jayne Mansfield, WILL SUCCESS SPOIL ROCK HUNTER?

—I can enjoy myself without it. I mean, not every time. I think it has to do with getting used to a man. Getting used to his body, position, the size. Oh, the size is great. The body's great.
—That just leaves position.
Brooke Adams and David Landsbury, GAS FOOD LODGING

—Come here. Come here.

—Yale . . .

—Lift your back leg.

—I don't have a back leg. Honey, it's our wedding night. It's not real romantic making love in the sink.

Albert Brooks and Goldie Hawn, PRIVATE BENJAMIN

—Oh, a hammock. That's so nostalgic. I lost it in a hammock. You really have to have good balance.

Julie Hagerty, A MIDSUMMER NIGHT'S SEX COMEDY

♥ ♥ ♥ ♥ ♥ ♥ Loneliness ♥ ♥ ♥ ♥ ♥ ♥

—Women are lonely in the nineties. It's our new phase.

Brooke Adams, GAS FOOD LODGING

—There's ten million people in this city alone. How difficult can it be to find one perfect person? It's not that big of a deal.

—I haven't, but maybe you can.

Albert Brooks and Bruno Kirby, MODERN ROMANCE

—On my prom night, I went around this park five times, six times. If I had been with a girl this would've been an incredible experience.

Woody Allen to Mariel Hemingway, MANHATTAN

♥ ♥ ♥ ♥ ♥ ♥ The Long Haul ♥ ♥ ♥ ♥ ♥ ♥

—Truth is pain and sweat and paying bills and making love to a woman that you don't love anymore.

Burl Ives, CAT ON A HOT TIN ROOF

—You know, when you're dating, everything is talking about sex, right? Where can we do it? You know, why can't we do it? . . . But then when you get married—it's crazy . . . I mean, you get it whenever you want it. You wake up in the morning and she's there, and you come home from work and she's there. And so all that sex-planning talk is over. And you have nothing to talk about.

Daniel Stern, DINER

♥ ♥ ♥ ♥ ♥ ♥ Love at First Sight ♥ ♥ ♥ ♥ ♥ ♥

—Do you believe in love at first sight?
—It saves a lot of time.

Ann Sheridan to George Raft, THEY DRIVE BY NIGHT

—I thought I was immune to movie stars. But I've wanted you from the first moment I saw you on screen and that never happens to me. You're the realist person I've ever met in the abstract. You're my fantasy, and I want to make you real. Let me love you.

Dennis Quaid to Meryl Streep, POSTCARDS FROM THE EDGE

—Do you believe in love at first sight? Yeah, I bet you don't. You're probably too sensible for that. Or, have you ever, like, seen somebody and you knew that, if only that person really knew you, they would, well of course, dump the perfect model that they were with, and realize that you were the one that they wanted to just grow old with?

Sandra Bullock to Peter Gallagher, WHILE YOU WERE SLEEPING

—I believe in animal attraction, I believe in love at first sight. I believe in *this*, and I don't feel it with you.

Ellen Barkin, snapping her fingers, to Al Pacino, SEA OF LOVE

Love-Hate
Relationships

♥ ♥ ♥ ♥ ♥ ♥   ♥ ♥ ♥ ♥ ♥ ♥

—I hate him.

—Hate? That's a pretty strong response for someone you said you didn't even like.

> Bonnie Hunt and Marisa Tomei, ONLY YOU

—Did you really think I was going to kill you, Martha?

—You kill me? That's a laugh.

—No, no, I might someday.

—Fat chance.

> Richard Burton and Elizabeth Taylor,
> WHO'S AFRAID OF VIRGINIA WOOLF?

—We go together, Laurie. I don't know why. Maybe like guns and ammunition go together.
John Dall to Peggy Cummins, GUN CRAZY

—With my brains and your looks, we could go places.
John Garfield to Audrey Trotter,
THE POSTMAN ALWAYS RINGS TWICE

—I killed him.
—I think what you did was so romantic.
Christian Slater and Patricia Arquette, TRUE ROMANCE

♥ ♥ ♥ ♥ ♥ ♥ Lovesick ♥ ♥ ♥ ♥ ♥ ♥

—I knew I was in love. First of all, I was very nauseous.

Woody Allen, TAKE THE MONEY AND RUN

—What do you do if every time you see this one incredible woman you think you're gonna hurl?

—I say, hurl. If you blow chunks and she comes back, she's yours. But if you spew and she bolts, it was never meant to be.

Dana Carvey to Mike Meyers, WAYNE'S WORLD

—I'm in love. It's great. I feel restless and I'm dizzy. It's wonderful. I bet I don't get any sleep tonight.

—That sounds more like indigestion.

Gordon John Sinclair and William Greenlees,
GREGORY'S GIRL

—I think I'm in love.

—Try to get some sleep, honey. You'll feel better in the morning.

Doris Day and Audrey Meadows, THAT TOUCH OF MINK

—Sometimes I feel things, Lucy.

—What you feel, I treat.

Ben Stiller and Sarah Jessica Parker, IF LUCY FELL

♥ ♥ ♥ ♥ ♥ ♥ Marital Advice ♥ ♥ ♥ ♥ ♥ ♥

—When the marriage goes to the rocks, the rocks are there—right there.

Judith Anderson, patting the bed, CAT ON A HOT TIN ROOF

—Make him feel important. If you do that, you'll have a happy and wonderful marriage—like two out of every ten couples.

Mildred Natwick to Jane Fonda, BAREFOOT IN THE PARK

—A wise woman patterns her life on the theories and practices of modern banking. She never gives her love, but only lends it on the best security and the highest rate of interest.

Jose Ferrer, MOULIN ROUGE

—The way most people go about it they use more brains picking a horse in the third at Belmont than they do picking a husband. It's your head you've got to use, not your heart.

Lauren Bacall, HOW TO MARRY A MILLIONAIRE

—No matter who you marry, you wake up married to someone else.

♥ ♥ ♥ ♥ ♥ ♥ Marriage ♥ ♥ ♥ ♥ ♥ ♥

—When it comes to marriage, one matters as good as the next. And even the least accommodating is less trouble than a mother.

Glenn Close to her ward, Uma Thurman, DANGEROUS LIAISONS

—Marriage is like a dull meal, with the dessert at the beginning.

Jose Ferrer, MOULIN ROUGE

— Marriage is a sacred thing, isn't it?
— In a beautiful, but sordid way.
  Lesley Ann Warren and Keith Carradine, CHOOSE ME

— Marriage is a good way to spend the winter.
  Edmund Gwenn, THE TROUBLE WITH HARRY

— I read in the *Enquirer* this morning that marriage causes cancer.
  Voice on radio, PRIVATE BENJAMIN

May-December
♥ ♥ ♥ ♥ ♥ ♥ Romances ♥ ♥ ♥ ♥ ♥ ♥

—Do you find me desirable?
—Oh, no, Mrs. Robinson. I think you're the most attractive of all my parents' friends.

Anne Bancroft and Dustin Hoffman, THE GRADUATE

—You don't think he's a little old?
—Oh, grow up, will ya? Men with that much dough are never a little old.

Betty Grable and Lauren Bacall, HOW TO MARRY A MILLIONAIRE

—Years from now when you talk about this—and you will—be kind.

Deborah Kerr to John Kerr, TEA AND SYMPATHY

♥ ♥ ♥ ♥ ♥ ♥ Men ♥ ♥ ♥ ♥ ♥ ♥

—He's like a spider, and he expects me to redecorate his web.

> Doris Day to Rock Hudson, PILLOW TALK

—There's no faith or trust or honesty in men.

> Pat Heywood, ROMEO AND JULIET

—Doesn't it ever enter a man's head that a woman can do without him?

> Ida Lupino to Cornel Wilde, ROAD HOUSE

—Men like to see women cry. It makes them feel superior.

> George Brent, THE SPIRAL STAIRCASE

—When women go wrong, men go right after them.
Mae West, SHE DONE HIM WRONG

—The only difference in men is the color of their neckties.
Ginger Rogers, TOP HAT

—If it didn't take men to make babies, I wouldn't have anything to do with any one of you.
Gena Rowlands, LONELY ARE THE BRAVE

♥ ♥ ♥ ♥ ♥ ♥ Mixed Messages ♥ ♥ ♥ ♥ ♥ ♥

—You begin to interest me . . . vaguely.
Dorothy Malone to Humphrey Bogart, THE BIG SLEEP

—I'd love to kiss ya, but I just washed my hair.
Bette Davis to Richard Barthelmess,
The CABIN IN THE COTTON

—You're not very tall, are you?
Carmen Sternwood to Humphrey Bogart, THE BIG SLEEP

♥ ♥ ♥ ♥ ♥ ♥ Monogamy ♥ ♥ ♥ ♥ ♥ ♥

—Oh, Daddy, what am I going to do?
—There's nothing you can do. If you want monogamy,
marry a swan.
Meryl Streep and Steve Hill, HEARTBURN

—I think people should mate for life, like pigeons or
Catholics.
Woody Allen, MANHATTAN

The Moon and the Stars

♥ ♥ ♥ ♥ ♥ ♥   ♥ ♥ ♥ ♥ ♥ ♥

—You want the moon? . . . Hey, that's a pretty good idea—I'll give you the moon, Mary.

James Stewart to Donna Reed, IT'S A WONDERFUL LIFE

—Don't let's ask for the moon. We have the stars.

Bette Davis to Paul Henreid, NOW, VOYAGER

—The stars will be jealous of you tonight. You are a vision.

Joaquin De Almeida to Marisa Tomei, ONLY YOU

—They didn't hit the moon with the first missile shot, either.

—I guess that's what I want, to hit the moon.

Tony Randall and Doris Day after kissing, PILLOW TALK

—I've never liked full moons; it gives people an excuse to act foolish.

Maya Angelou, HOW TO MAKE AN AMERICAN QUILT

—You just wished on a planet.

—Figures.

Christian Slater and Marisa Tomei, UNTAMED HEART

—It wasn't the first time I went to bed with a guy and woke up with a note.

Susan Sarandon, BULL DURHAM

—Sex changes things. I've had relationships where I know a guy and then I have sex with him and then I bump into him someplace and he acts like I loaned him money.

Teri Garr, TOOTSIE

—I know exactly how you feel, my dear. The morning after always looks grim if you happen to be wearing last night's dress.

Ina Claire, NINOTCHKA

♥ ♥ ♥ ♥ ♥ ♥ Not the Marrying ♥ ♥ ♥ ♥ ♥ ♥
Kind

—She tried to sit in my lap while I was standing up.
Humphrey Bogart, THE BIG SLEEP

—Do I ice her? Do I marry her? Which one of these?
—Marry her, Charlie. Just because she's a thief and a hitter doesn't mean she's not a good woman in all the other departments.
Jack Nicholson and Anjelica Huston, PRIZZI'S HONOR

—I have heard so much about you.
—Yeah, but you can't prove it.
Gilbert Roland and Mae West, SHE DONE HIM WRONG

♥ ♥ ♥ ♥ ♥ ♥ Obsession ♥ ♥ ♥ ♥ ♥ ♥

—Don't you think it's better for a girl to be preoccupied with sex than occupied?
Maggie McNamara, THE MOON IS BLUE

—Is sex all you ever think about?
—Other thoughts creep in; I just ignore them.
Lewis Alante and Slade Burrus, THE BOYS OF CELLBLOCK Q

♥ ♥ ♥ ♥ ♥ ♥ The Oldest Profession ♥ ♥ ♥ ♥ ♥ ♥

—Are you a hooker? Jesus, I forgot. I just thought I was doing great with you.
Dudley Moore, ARTHUR

—I appreciate this whole seduction scene you've got going here, but let me give you a tip: I'm a sure thing.
Julia Roberts to Richard Gere, PRETTY WOMAN

—Some men are paying two hundred dollars for me and here you are turning down a freebee.
Jane Fonda to Donald Sutherland, KLUTE

—I'm a hooker. You're a trick. Why ruin a perfect relationship?
Kathleen Turner to Anthony Perkins, CRIMES OF PASSION

—I may be a prostitute, but I am not promiscuous.
Barbra Streisand, THE OWL AND THE PUSSYCAT

♥ ♥ ♥ ♥ ♥ ♥ On the Rocks ♥ ♥ ♥ ♥ ♥ ♥

—What do you call it when you hate the woman you love?
—A wife.

> Jack Lemmon and Eddie Mayehoff,
> HOW TO MURDER YOUR WIFE

—I swear, if you existed I'd divorce you.

> Elizabeth Taylor to Richard Burton,
> WHO'S AFRAID OF VIRGINIA WOOLF?

♥ ♥ ♥ ♥ ♥ ♥ Opposite Sex ♥ ♥ ♥ ♥ ♥ ♥

—Look at that! Look how she moves. It looks just like Jell-O on springs. Must have some sort of built-in motor or something. I tell you, it's a whole different sex.

Jack Lemmon, referring to Marilyn Monroe, SOME LIKE IT HOT

—I could never be a woman. I would just stay at home and play with my breasts all day.

Steve Martin, L.A. STORY

♥ ♥ ♥ ♥ ♥ ♥ Orgasms ♥ ♥ ♥ ♥ ♥ ♥

—I finally had an orgasm and my doctor told me it was the wrong kind.

—I never had the wrong kind . . . My worst one was right on the money.

Party guest and Woody Allen, MANHATTAN

—I haven't had an orgasm like that in nine and a half years. I never thought I was capable of this. I'm ashamed of myself. I am. Glad and ashamed. Exhausted and exhilarated all at the same time. Just as I was repelled and attracted to you at the same time. Yin and yang, you understand?

Bette Midler, DOWN AND OUT IN BEVERLY HILLS

—Once when I was with my first husband, I got to this place that was nice and tingly, and I don't know if this was an official orgasm, but I counted it as one for five years.

Goldie Hawn, PRIVATE BENJAMIN

—Now I know what I've been faking all these years.

Goldie Hawn, PRIVATE BENJAMIN

—I finally understand what the fuss is all about.

Geena Davis after spending the night with Brad Pitt,
THELMA & LOUISE

—I'll have what she's having.

Customer in diner to waiter after watching Meg Ryan
fake an orgasm at the next table, WHEN HARRY MET SALLY . . .

♥♥♥♥♥♥ The Pain of Love ♥♥♥♥♥♥

—It was only when I began to feel actual physical pain every time you left the room that it finally dawned on me: I was in love.

John Malkovich to Michelle Pfeiffer, DANGEROUS LIAISONS

—To love is to suffer. Not to love is to suffer. To suffer is to suffer.

Woody Allen, LOVE AND DEATH

—Why be miserable with someone you don't love? It's better to be miserable with someone you do love.

Gina Lollobrigida, COME SEPTEMBER

♥ ♥ ♥ ♥ ♥ ♥ Parting Is Such ♥ ♥ ♥ ♥ ♥ ♥
Sweet Sorrow

—If that plane leaves the ground and you're not with him, you'll regret it. Maybe not today, and maybe not tomorrow, but soon and for the rest of your life.

Humphrey Bogart to Ingrid Bergman, CASABLANCA

—I have to leave you now. I'm going to that corner there and turn. You must stay in the car and drive away. Promise not to watch me go beyond the corner. Just drive away and leave me as I leave you.

Audrey Hepburn to Gregory Peck, ROMAN HOLIDAY

♥ ♥ ♥ ♥ ♥ ♥ Passion ♥ ♥ ♥ ♥ ♥ ♥

—Everything seems like nothing to me now. Except that I want you in my bed. I don't care if I burn in hell. I don't care if you burn in hell. The past and the future is a joke to me now. I see that they're nothing. I see they ain't here. The only thing that's here is you and me.

Nicolas Cage to Cher, MOONSTRUCK

—Why do you have to look so beautiful? You're getting married in an hour. Another dream shot. And if that wasn't enough, you've got to come in here looking like a convention of angels. Why does the sunlight have to hit you just right? If your nose was shiny or your eyes were dull—anything to make it easier. But look at you.

—Well, a girl can't get married without a permanent, can she? It wouldn't be legal.

Frank Sinatra and Doris Day, YOUNG AT HEART

—How can one change an entire life and build a new one in a moment of love, and yet that's what you make me want to close my eyes and do.
Greta Garbo to Robert Taylor, CAMILLE

♥ ♥ ♥ ♥ ♥ ♥ Philosophy of ♥ ♥ ♥ ♥ ♥ ♥ Love

—Those who are most worthy of love are never made happy by it.
Mildred Natwick, DANGEROUS LIAISONS

—Can love really be satisfied with such polite affections? To love is to burn.
Kate Winslet to Emma Thompson, SENSE AND SENSIBILITY

—When in doubt, fuck.

Al Pacino, Scent of a Woman

—Nothing worth knowing can be understood with the mind. Everything really valuable has to enter you through a different opening.

Woody Allen, Manhattan

—I kept asking Clarence why our world kept collapsing and everything seemed so shitty and he'd say, "That's the way it goes. But don't forget, it goes the other way, too." That's the way romance goes. But every once in a while, it goes the other way, too.

Patricia Arquette, True Romance

—For me love has to go very deep. Sex only has to go a few inches.

Stacey Nelkin, Bullets Over Broadway

♥ ♥ ♥ ♥ ♥ ♥ Playing Coy ♥ ♥ ♥ ♥ ♥ ♥

—This is very unusual. I've never been alone with a man before, even with my dress on. With my dress off, it's most unusual. I don't seem to mind. Do you?

Audrey Hepburn to Gregory Peck, ROMAN HOLIDAY

—I can never get a zipper to close. Maybe that stands for something. What do you think?

Rita Hayworth to Glenn Ford, GILDA

—I'm not hard to get, Steve. All you have to do is ask me.

Lauren Bacall to Humphrey Bogart, TO HAVE AND HAVE NOT

—I was nowhere near your neighborhood and I saw your light on. Can I come in?

Campbell Scott to Kyra Sedgwick, SINGLES

♥ ♥ ♥ ♥ ♥ ♥ Poets ♥ ♥ ♥ ♥ ♥ ♥

—And when [her lips] touched yours they were like that first swallow of wine after you just crossed the desert.

Al Pacino, SCENT OF A WOMAN

—Every woman is a mystery to be solved, but a woman hides nothing from a true lover. Her skin color can tell us how to proceed. A hue like the blush of a rose, pink and pale. And she must be coaxed to open her petals with the warmth like the sun.

Johnny Depp, DON JUAN DEMARCO

—I live alone, within myself, like a hut within the woods. I keep my heart high up on the shelf, barren of other goods. I need another's arms to reach for it and place it where it belongs. I need another's touch and smile to fill my hut with songs.

William Hickey, SEA OF LOVE

♥ ♥ ♥ ♥ ♥ ♥ Polygamy ♥ ♥ ♥ ♥ ♥ ♥

—One wife? One God, that I can understand—but one wife! That is not civilized. It is not generous.

Jack Hawkins, BEN-HUR

—You love this woman enough to ask her to be your wife and the mother of my children. And that takes a lot of love. You sure you don't love her?

—The moment I saw you downstairs I knew . . .

—Oh, go on, I bet you say that to all your wives.

Irene Dunne and Cary Grant, MY FAVORITE WIFE

♥ ♥ ♥ ♥ ♥ ♥ Popping the ♥ ♥ ♥ ♥ ♥ ♥
Question

—I'm asking you to marry me, you little fool.
Laurence Olivier to Olivia De Havilland, REBECCA

—Do you think after we've dried off, after we've spent lots more time together, you might agree *not* to marry me? And do you think *not* being married to me might maybe be something you could consider doing for the rest of your life? Do you?
—I do.

Hugh Grant and Andie MacDowell,
FOUR WEDDINGS AND A FUNERAL

—No more Mr. Nice Guy. I want an answer and I want it now.

—Is that a threat?

—No, it's a proposal.

Tim Matheson and Kate Capshaw, A LITTLE SEX

—Marry me.

—Why?

—I want you around in the morning.

—I'm already around in the morning.

—I want to know you're legally required to be there.

Michelle Pfeiffer and Robert Redford,

UP CLOSE & PERSONAL

♥ ♥ ♥ ♥ ♥ ♥ Propositions ♥ ♥ ♥ ♥ ♥ ♥

—Mrs. Robinson, you're trying to seduce me . . . aren't you?

> Dustin Hoffman to Ann Bancroft, THE GRADUATE

—Want to get your paws full of honey, you sad funny bear?

> Mary Woronov,
> SCENES FROM THE CLASS STRUGGLE IN BEVERLY HILLS

—You can either watch me or join me. One of them's more fun.

> Peter O'Toole, MY FAVORITE YEAR

—Come on, darling. Why don't you kick off your spurs?

Elizabeth Taylor inviting Rock Hudson to bed, GIANT

—Gimme some sugar, baby.

Bruce Campbell to Embeth Davidtz, ARMY OF DARKNESS

—It's going to be a long night . . . and I don't particularly like the book I started.

Eva Marie Saint to Cary Grant, NORTH BY NORTHWEST

—How about coming up to my place for a spot of heavy breathing?

Walter Matthau to Carol Burnett, PETE 'N' TILLY

—Any time you got nothin' to do and lots of time to do it, come on up.

Mae West, SHE DONE HIM WRONG

♥♥♥♥♥♥ Relationships ♥♥♥♥♥♥

—Maybe people weren't meant to have one deep relationship. Maybe we're meant to have, you know, a series of relationships of different lengths. I mean, that kind of thing's gone out of date.

Mariel Hemingway to Woody Allen, MANHATTAN

—It's perfectly normal in a healthy relationship to give up some of your own identity.

—Well, I don't want to do that, because I don't have any extra.

Mia Farrow and Sarah Jessica Parker, MIAMI RHAPSODY

—What is a "proper relationship"?
—Living with someone who talks to you after they
banged you.

Katrin Cartlidge and Lesley Sharp, NAKED

♥ ♥ ♥ ♥ ♥ ♥ Repartee ♥ ♥ ♥ ♥ ♥ ♥

—I always have liked redheads.
—You shouldn't. Red means stop.
—I'm color-blind.

George Raft and Ann Sheridan, THEY DRIVE BY NIGHT

—I didn't know you were so small.
—I'm taller than Napoleon.
—You're prettier too.

Robert Mitchum and Jane Greer, OUT OF THE PAST

—Speaking of horses . . . you've got a touch of class, but I don't know how far you can go.

—A lot depends on who's in the saddle. Go ahead, Marlowe. I like the way you work. In case you don't know it, you're doing all right.

Humphrey Bogart and Lauren Bacall, THE BIG SLEEP

—Maybe you think I've been trying too hard to get acquainted.

—Maybe you have.

—Maybe you think that's wrong.

—Maybe it's too soon to tell.

Lizabeth Scott and Van Heflin,
THE STRANGE LOVE OF MARTHA IVERS

—My temperature runs a little high . . . I don't mind. It's the engine or something.

—Maybe you need a tune-up.

—Don't tell me, you have just the right tool.
Kathleen Turner and William Hurt, BODY HEAT

♥ ♥ ♥ ♥ ♥ ♥ The Screen Kiss ♥ ♥ ♥ ♥ ♥ ♥

—Was that cannon fire, or is it my heart pounding?
Ingrid Bergman to Humphrey Bogart, CASABLANCA

—I like that. I'd like more.
Lauren Bacall to Humphrey Bogart, THE BIG SLEEP

—That was restful. Again.
  Greta Garbo, learning to kiss, NINOTCHKA

♥ ♥ ♥ ♥ ♥ ♥ Second Marriages ♥ ♥ ♥ ♥ ♥ ♥

—I'm one of the most faithful husbands that ever lived.
—With a wife in every room.
  Cary Grant and Irene Dunne, MY FAVORITE WIFE

—I want to extend my compliments to the bridesmaids. You did your duties superbly, and obviously I plan to use your services every time I get married from now on.
  Corin Redgrave, FOUR WEDDINGS AND A FUNERAL

—I want you three to be bridesmaids.

—What happened to the ones you used the last time?

—I never use the same bridesmaids twice; it's bad luck.

Lainie Kazan and Olympia Dukakis, THE CEMETERY CLUB

—Why don't I get married again? I don't get married again because I can't find anyone I dislike enough to inflict that kind of torture on.

Roy Scheider, ALL THAT JAZZ

♥ ♥ ♥ ♥ ♥ ♥ Security ♥ ♥ ♥ ♥ ♥ ♥

—In spite of the fact that all men are males, there's no feeling so secure as having a good reliable husband.

Helen Broderick, TOP HAT

—Why would a guy want to marry another guy?
—Security.

Tony Curtis and Jack Lemmon, SOME LIKE IT HOT

♥ ♥ ♥ ♥ ♥ ♥ Seduction ♥ ♥ ♥ ♥ ♥ ♥

—There are some women, fine-featured, a certain texture to the hair, a curve to the ear that sweeps like the turn of a shell. These women have fingers with the same sensitivities as their legs. The fingertips are the same feelings as their feet. And when you touch their knuckles, it is like passing your hands around their knees. And this tender fleshy part of the finger, is the same as brushing your hands around their thighs. And, finally . . . [kisses her hand.]

Johnny Depp, DON JUAN DEMARCO

♥ ♥ ♥ ♥ ♥ ♥ Self-Love ♥ ♥ ♥ ♥ ♥ ♥

— Have you ever been in love?
— Yes, for as long as I can remember — with myself.
Laurence Harvey and Julie Christie, DARLING

— I look so incredibly handsome with a cigarette.
Woody Allen, MANHATTAN

—The truth is, unlike you, I never expected the thunderbolt. I always just hoped that I would meet some nice, friendly girl and like the look of her and hope the look of me didn't make her physically sick and pop the question and settle down and be happy. It worked for my parents, apart from the divorce and all that.

James Fleet, FOUR WEDDINGS AND A FUNERAL

—I don't ask much, do I? I mean I don't ask to be famous, and I don't ask to be rich, and I don't ask to play center field for the New York Yankees, or anything. I just want to meet a woman, and I want to fall in love, and I want to get married, and I want to have a kid, and I want to go see him play a tooth in the school play. It's not much.

Tom Hanks, SPLASH

♥ ♥ ♥ ♥ ♥ ♥ Sex ♥ ♥ ♥ ♥ ♥ ♥

—I hear that relationships that begin under intense circumstances never last.
—OK. We'll have to base ours on sex then.
Keanu Reeves and Sandra Bullock, SPEED

—That was the most fun I've had without laughing.
Woody Allen, ANNIE HALL

—I thought sentiment made you uncomfortable.
—I can handle it, as long as it's disguised as sex.
Margaret Colin and Tom Selleck, THREE MEN AND A BABY

Sexual
Performance

♥ ♥ ♥ ♥ ♥ ♥   ♥ ♥ ♥ ♥ ♥ ♥

—I was incredible last night in bed. I never once had to sit up and consult the manual.

  Woody Allen, PLAY IT AGAIN, SAM

—I'm at my sexual peak. Once a guy hits eighteen, it's all downhill.

—But it's a lovely ride.

  Ken Olandt and Mark Harmon, SUMMER SCHOOL

—I am putty in your hands.

—In my hands nothing turns to putty.

Charlie Sheen and Brenda Bakke, HOT SHOTS! PART DEUX

—The only people who make love all the time are liars.

Louis Jourdan, GIGI

—You made a woman meow?

Bruno Kirby to Billy Crystal, WHEN HARRY MET SALLY . . .

♥ ♥ ♥ ♥ ♥ ♥ Short and Sweet ♥ ♥ ♥ ♥ ♥ ♥

—You said you loved me.
—I meant it at the time.
—Well, what is it, a viral love? Kind of a twenty-four-hour thing?

Meryl Streep and Dennis Quaid, POSTCARDS FROM THE EDGE

—I need tending, I need someone to take care of me, someone to rub my tired muscles, smooth out the sheets.

—Get married.

—I just need it for tonight.

William Hurt and Kathleen Turner, BODY HEAT

—Just remember that every relationship starts with a one-night stand.

Anthony Edwards, THE SURE THING

♥ ♥ ♥ ♥ ♥ ♥ The Single Life ♥ ♥ ♥ ♥ ♥ ♥

—If there is anything worse than a woman living alone, it's a woman saying she likes it.

Thelma Ritter, PILLOW TALK

—This is what single people do. They try other people on and see how they fit. But everybody's an adjustment. Nobody's perfect. There's no such thing as perfect . . .

Tom Hanks, SLEEPLESS IN SEATTLE

—If I wanted a man in my life, I wouldn't have bought a VCR.

Michelle Pfeiffer, FRANKIE AND JOHNNY

♥ ♥ ♥ ♥ ♥ ♥ Slapping and ♥ ♥ ♥ ♥ ♥ ♥
Being Slapped

—That's for making me care about you.

Andie MacDowell to Bill Murray, GROUNDHOG DAY

—When you're slapped, you'll take it and like it.
  Humphrey Bogart to Peter Lorre, THE MALTESE FALCON

—Don't do that again. For me, it isn't erotic.
  Christopher Eigeman to Isabel Gillies, METROPOLITAN

—That slap in the face you took . . . Well, you hardly
blinked an eye. It takes a lot of practice to be able to do that.
  Humphrey Bogart to Lauren Bacall, TO HAVE AND HAVE NOT

♥ ♥ ♥ ♥ ♥ ♥ Sleeping Around ♥ ♥ ♥ ♥ ♥ ♥

—Of course, I may bring a boyfriend home occasionally. But only occasionally. Because I do think that one
ought to go to the man's room if one can. I mean, it
doesn't look so much as one expected it. Does it?
  Liza Minnelli, CABARET

—After a lifetime of marriage, to suddenly be in a relationship where I'm in control . . . to feel sexy again. Maybe
I should have done it years ago.
—No, you know, it's good you waited. It's the perfect
moment in medical history to turn promiscuous.

Mia Farrow and Sarah Jessica Parker, MIAMI RHAPSODY

—Provided you take a few elementary precautions,
you can do it or not with as many men as you like, as often
as you like, in as many different ways as you like. Our sex
has few enough advantages, you may as well make the
best of those you have.

Glenn Close, DANGEROUS LIAISONS

—I think it's true the height of the sexual revolution is
over. I don't go to bed with just anyone anymore—I have
to be attracted to them sexually.

Mira Sorvino, BARCELONA

—Haven't you ever met a man that could make you happy?

—Sure, lots of times.

Cary Grant and Mae West, SHE DONE HIM WRONG

♥ ♥ ♥ ♥ ♥ Smart Women, ♥ ♥ ♥ ♥ ♥ ♥
Foolish Choices

—He's shifty as smoke, but I love him.

Thelma Ritter, PICKUP ON SOUTH STREET

—I've gone out with some bums in my day, but they were beautiful. That is the only reason to go out with a bum.

Mercedes Ruehl, THE FISHER KING

—I don't know what to do with you. You're a nice guy.

Amy Irving to Peter Riegert, CROSSING DELANCEY

—There are a lot of men out there. I'm selective. I look around very carefully, and when I find the one I think can give me the worst possible time, that's when I make my move.

Jessica Lange, TOOTSIE

♥ ♥ ♥ ♥ ♥ ♥ Smooth Moves ♥ ♥ ♥ ♥ ♥ ♥

—Never let on how much you like a girl. Wherever you are, act like it's the place to be. You call the shots. When ordering, find out what she wants, then order for the both of you. It's a classy move. This is most important of all. When it comes down to making out, whenever possible, put on side one of *Led Zeppelin IV*.

Robert Romanus, FAST TIMES AT RIDGEMONT HIGH

—What could I offer her?
—There's the usual: flowers, chocolates, promises you don't intend to keep.

Robby Benson as the Beast and David Ogden Stiers as Cogsworth, BEAUTY AND THE BEAST

Someday My Prince
♥ ♥ ♥ ♥ ♥ ♥ Will Come ♥ ♥ ♥ ♥ ♥ ♥

—This is no ordinary apple. It's a magic wishing apple
. . . One bite and all your dreams will come true.
—Really?
—Yes, girlie. Now, make a wish and take a bite.

Lucille la Verne as the Queen and Adriana Caselotti as
Snow White, SNOW WHITE AND THE SEVEN DWARFS

—Oh, well, what's a royal ball? After all, I suppose it
would be frightfully dull and boring, and completely . . .
completely wonderful.

Ilene Woods as Cinderella, CINDERELLA

—You'll come out or I'll break down the door.

—Master, I could be wrong, but that may not be the best way to win the girl's affection.

Robby Benson as the Beast and Jerry Orbach as Lumiere,
BEAUTY AND THE BEAST

♥ ♥ ♥ ♥ ♥ ♥ Stolen Hearts ♥ ♥ ♥ ♥ ♥ ♥

—If you take my heart by surprise, the rest of my body has the right to follow.

Albert Finney, TOM JONES

—You don't do this to a person, you know. You don't walk around being fabulous when you know you're not available.

Billy Crystal to Debra Winger, FORGET PARIS

♥ ♥ ♥ ♥ ♥ ♥ Sweet Nothings ♥ ♥ ♥ ♥ ♥ ♥

—It's midnight. Look at the clock. One hand has met the other hand. They kiss. Isn't that wonderful?

Melvyn Douglas to Greta Garbo, NINOTCHKA

—You fell in love with me because . . .
—Because I began to hear music again.

Andie MacDowell and Gerard Depardieu, GREEN CARD

137

—I was born when you kissed me. I died when you left me. I lived a few weeks while you loved me.

Gloria Grahame to Humphrey Bogart, IN A LONELY PLACE

—I get a nice warm feeling being near you, ma'am. It's like being round a pot-bellied stove on a frosty morning.

Rock Hudson to Doris Day, PILLOW TALK

—Who are you?
—Who, me? I'm the whippoorwill that cries in the night. I'm the soft morning breeze that caresses your lovely face.

Claudette Colbert and Clark Gable, IT HAPPENED ONE NIGHT

Till Death
♥ ♥ ♥ ♥ ♥ ♥ ♥ ♥ ♥ ♥ ♥ ♥
Do Us Part

—Would you hang us together, please?
> Katharine Hepburn about Humphrey Bogart,
> THE AFRICAN QUEEN

—Someone has killed herself for love of you. I do wish that I had had such an experience. The women who have admired me . . . have all insisted on living on long after I had ceased to care for them.
> George Sanders, THE PICTURE OF DORIAN GRAY

—You came for me! You're alive!
—I would die for you.
> Mary Elizabeth Mastrantonio and Kevin Costner,
> ROBIN HOOD: PRINCE OF THIEVES

—You smell good, Myra. Like a bitch in a hothouse.
—Oh, darling. What a beautiful thing to say.
    John Cusack and Annette Bening, THE GRIFTERS

—Hey, that's a nice perfume.
—Something new. Attracts mosquitoes and repels men.

    Lee Marvin and Gloria Grahame, THE BIG HEAT

♥ ♥ ♥ ♥ ♥ ♥ True Love ♥ ♥ ♥ ♥ ♥ ♥

—Have you never met a woman who inspires you to love, until your every sense is filled with her? You inhale her. You test her. You see your unborn children in her eyes. And know that your heart has at last found a home. Your life begins with her, and without her, it must surely end.

Johnny Depp, DON JUAN DEMARCO

—I love the lady and will continue to love her forever. If she were on one side of the globe and I on the other, I would pierce through the whole mass of the world to reach her.

Nick Nolte, JEFFERSON IN PARIS

—It's love, fellows. I met the girl. She's . . . I can't describe her, but the first thing you notice are those dimples when she smiles. I found her. I didn't think they came that way anymore. She's sweet, intelligent, a perfect playmate.

Cary Grant, HOLIDAY

—It was a million tiny little things that when you add them all up, it just meant that we were supposed to be together, and I knew it. I knew it the very first time that I touched her. It was like coming home. Only to no home I'd ever known. I was just taking her hand to help her out of a car, and I knew it. It was like magic.

Tom Hanks, SLEEPLESS IN SEATTLE

♥ ♥ ♥ ♥ ♥ ♥ Virgins ♥ ♥ ♥ ♥ ♥ ♥

—Men are usually so bored with virgins. I'm so glad you're not.

Maggie McNamara, THE MOON IS BLUE

—I am just not interested in doing it until I find the right person. You see how picky I am about my shoes, and they only go on my feet.

Alicia Silverstone, CLUELESS

—The PC term is "hymenly challenged."

Stacy Dash, CLUELESS

—She's harder to get into than a Pearl Jam concert.

Jack Noseworthy, THE BRADY BUNCH MOVIE

♥ ♥ ♥ ♥ ♥ ♥ We Can Still ♥ ♥ ♥ ♥ ♥ ♥
Be Friends

—Are you still on speaking terms with your last husband?

—Oh, sure, I never let a divorce break up a friendship.

Linda Darnell and Binnie Barnes, DAYTIME WIFE

—It's so refreshing to hear a man speak so highly of the woman he's divorcing.

Monica Evans, THE ODD COUPLE

—Aren't we still friends?

—No, we are not friends. I don't take this shit from friends—only from lovers.

Dustin Hoffman and Teri Garr, TOOTSIE

—I'll miss you, we'll talk, we'll always be friends. We'll get hot for each other every few years at dinner and we'll never act on it. Okay. I got to go.
Albert Brooks to Holly Hunter, BROADCAST NEWS

♥ ♥ ♥ ♥ ♥ ♥ Weddings ♥ ♥ ♥ ♥ ♥ ♥

—Well, good luck. It's pretty easy, just say "I do" whenever anyone asks you a question.
Andie MacDowell to Hugh Grant,
FOUR WEDDINGS AND A FUNERAL

—I now pronounce you men and wives.
Ian Wolfe, SEVEN BRIDES FOR SEVEN BROTHERS

—If you're going to invest two dollars in a marriage license, you should get your money's worth.
Betsy Drake, WILL SUCCESS SPOIL ROCK HUNTER?

—Will thou love her?
—From the bottom of my soul to the tip of my penis — like a sun in its brightness, the moon in its glory.
Alastair Sim and Peter O'Toole, THE RULING CLASS

♥ ♥ ♥ ♥ ♥ ♥ Widows ♥ ♥ ♥ ♥ ♥ ♥

—There's one good thing in being a widow, isn't there? You don't have to ask your husband for money.
Frances Carson to Joseph Cotten, SHADOW OF A DOUBT

—If someone is a widower, why do they say that he was widowed? Why don't they say he was widowered? I was just wondering.

Meg Ryan, SLEEPLESS IN SEATTLE

♥ ♥ ♥ ♥ ♥ ♥ A Woman of Virtue ♥ ♥ ♥ ♥ ♥ ♥

—To seduce a woman famous for strict morals, religious fervor, and the happiness of her marriage, what could possibly be more prestigious?

John Malkovich, DANGEROUS LIAISONS

—You have rare qualities. You're direct, sincere, uncomplicated. You're the type of woman who brings out the worst in a man: his conscience.

Cary Grant, THAT TOUCH OF MINK

—The minute I saw her I knew this was no ordinary woman. There was something about her . . . purity, innocence, honor.

—All the virtues that drive a man to drink.

Gig Young and Cary Grant, THAT TOUCH OF MINK

♥ ♥ ♥ ♥ ♥ ♥ A Woman's Charm ♥ ♥ ♥ ♥ ♥ ♥

—Fidelity is a fading woman's protection and a charming woman's weakness.

Douglas Fairbanks, Jr., THE PRISONER OF ZENDA

—I know I fib a good deal. After all, a woman's charm is fifty percent illusion.

Vivien Leigh, A STREETCAR NAMED DESIRE

♥ ♥ ♥ ♥ ♥ ♥ Women ♥ ♥ ♥ ♥ ♥ ♥

—All women are wonders because they reduce all men to the obvious.

Ken Niles, OUT OF THE PAST

—There are two kinds of women: high maintenance and low maintenance. You're the worst kind. You're high maintenance, but you think you're low maintenance.

Billy Crystal to Meg Ryan, WHEN HARRY MET SALLY . . .

—Women make the best psychoanalysts till they fall in love. After that, they make the best patients.

Ingrid Bergman, SPELLBOUND

—How extravagant you are, throwing away women like that. Someday they may be scarce.

Claude Rains to Humphrey Bogart, CASABLANCA

—As many times as I'll be married, I'll never understand women.

Tony Randall, PILLOW TALK

—Do you know what she has done to me? It's terrible. She's turned me into an honest man.

Fritz Wepper, CABARET

—When you make it with some of these chicks, they think you gotta dance with them.

John Travolta, SATURDAY NIGHT FEVER

—I treated her like a pair of gloves. When I was cold, I called her up.

Cornel Wilde, THE BIG COMBO

—You married?

—Occasionally. I'm always on the lookout for a future ex–Mrs. Malcolm.

Sam Neill and Jeff Goldblum, JURASSIC PARK

You Kiss with That Mouth?

♥ ♥ ♥ ♥ ♥ ♥   ♥ ♥ ♥ ♥ ♥ ♥

—Nola, just let me smell it. Please baby, please baby, please baby, baby baby please.

Spike Lee to Tracy Camila, SHE'S GOTTA HAVE IT

—Legs, I don't care if they're Greek columns or secondhand Steinways, what's between 'em is the passport to heaven. Yes, there are only two syllables in this whole wide world worth hearing: pus-sy.

Al Pacino, SCENT OF A WOMAN

—What the fuck. If you can't say it, you can't do it.

Richard Masur, RISKY BUSINESS

—I have no balls. All I have is a set of fat, petty dictators sewn up in cheap leather. A couple of greedy monsters dangling in a smarmy woman's purse. The kind you buy at Kmart. Monogamy was my kingdom, and they have exiled me.

Wallace Shawn,
SCENES FROM THE CLASS STRUGGLE IN BEVERLY HILLS

You Say the Sweetest Things

♥ ♥ ♥ ♥ ♥ ♥   ♥ ♥ ♥ ♥ ♥ ♥

—There's a magnificence in you, Tracy . . . a magnificence that comes out of your eyes and your voice and the way you stand there and the way you walk. You're lit from within, Tracy. You've got fires banked down in you, hearth fires and holocausts.

James Stewart to Katharine Hepburn, THE PHILADELPHIA STORY

—You have perfection about you. Your eyes have music. Your heart's the best part of your body. And when you move, every man, woman, and child is forced to watch.

Keith Carradine to Lesley Ann Warren, CHOOSE ME

—I love that you get cold when it's seventy-one degrees out. I love that it takes you an hour and a half to order a sandwich. I love that you get a little crinkle above your nose when you're looking at me like I'm nuts. I love that after I spend a day with you I can still smell your perfume on my clothes. And I love that you are the last person I want to talk to before I go to sleep at night.

Billy Crystal to Meg Ryan, WHEN HARRY MET SALLY . . .